Copyright

© 2014 Rose J. Fresquez

All rights reserved. This book or any portion thereof

may not be reproduced or used in any manner whatsoever

without the express written permission of the publisher

except for the use of brief quotations in a book review, magazine, church group or broadcasts.

Printed in the United States of America

First Printing, 2014

ISBN 978-1500392116

Published by Rose J. Fresquez

Printed by Createspace, an amazon.com Company

Dedication:

I dedicate this book to my three children, Isaiah, Caleb and Abigail. They constantly remind me of God's love and patience as we journey through life. It is through their questions about God; who He is, why we can't see Him, why we worship God and other questions such as these which led me to a journey of research and inspiration to write this book.

With much thanks to the following people for their support and inspiration: Laura Krokos, Melissa Rice, Candace Wright, Kathy Miskie, Karen Bransgrove, Karyn Suppes, Jerri Hall, Phillip, Barbara and all my Fresquez family, my wonderful small group and church family at Riverside Church. I give extra thanks to my husband Joel, who works so hard so that I can be a home maker and author.

Most of all, I give praise to the Lord for standing by my side always and strengthening me to do anything through Christ. Philippians 4:13

The Ten Commandments For Kids and Families
A 12-WEEK FAMILY DEVOTIONAL FOR LEADING HEARTS TO CHRIST

PARENTS:

Dear parents,

It's such a great joy and gift to raise your children and watch them grow especially in the Lord. As Psalm 127:3-4 says, "Children are a blessing from the Lord, offspring a reward from him. Like arrows in the hands of a warrior are children born in one's youth."

The most important gift you can give to your children is teaching them the love and fear of God. If it were not for my mom, I would never have come to know of Jesus and what He did for me on the cross.

When my mom accepted Christ as her personal savior, her whole life was transformed from the inside out. She was so passionate about the Lord, and yes, you could tell that something was very different in her. She was one you would call a contagious Christian, inspiring everyone around her.

Not only should you teach your children about God, but like a role model should, you must live what you teach them. Kids learn more by observing what their role model does than what they are being told to do.

Our job as parents is not to transform our kids' lives to Christ, it is to teach them. Only God has the power to change their hearts. We can only teach and then pray for them to understand and know God through His son Jesus, at a personal level.

It all starts with the Ten Commandments. This is God's law which will help your children understand that we are all sinners and far from God's standard. Unless they realize and understand being a sinner, they will never feel the need for a savior and cannot understand God's grace.

We were given these 10 basic rules for our own good, learning and growth. If we can instill these 10 Commandments in our children, explaining their depth and complexities, our kids will become happier adults desiring godliness rather than worldliness.

"Impress them on your children. Talk about them when you sit at home and when you walk along the road, when you lie down and when you get up. Tie them as symbols on your hands and bind them on your foreheads. Write them on the doorframes of your houses and on your gates. " Deuteronomy 6:7

Guidelines:

This book is designed for family devotions, one chapter a week. Choose the best day and time of the week, to go through one commandment at a time. Then, review it along with Bible stories and verses through the week. This will help your children to understand it better without rushing through the book. You could break one Commandment into several sections. One day you could talk about a given Commandment and what it means and then go through the supporting verses and activity on a different day. Do whatever works best for your family and your schedule.

TABLE OF CONTENTS

THE TEN COMMANDMENTS..6

- What are the Ten Commandments?
- How and why we got the Ten Commandments?
- What to do with the Ten Commandments
- Purpose of the Ten Commandments

FIRST COMMANDMENT..11

- What does it mean to have no other gods before God?
- What is a god?
- What happens when we put God first?
- Lesson of Daniel in the Lion's Den

SECOND COMMANDMENT..18

- What is an idol?
- What does it mean to have an image in the form of anything?
- What happens when we worship idols?
- Why should God alone be worshipped?
- Lesson of Elijah on Mount Carmel

THIRD COMMANDMENT..27

- What is the meaning of a name?
- Why should we respect God's name?
- What names of God are revealed in the Bible?
- What are some ways in which we don't respect God's name?

FOURTH COMMANDMENT..32

- What is the Sabbath?
- How can we can keep the Sabbath holy?
- Lesson of Manna from Heaven

FIFTH COMMANDMENT..38

- What does honor mean?
- What are some ways you can honor your parents?

- Why should we obey our parents?

- Lesson of how Jesus honored his parents

SIXTH COMMANDMENT 45

- What is murder?
- Lesson of Cain and Abel

SEVENTH COMMANDMENT 51

- Lesson of David and Bathsheba

EIGHT COMMANDMENT 57

- What is stealing?
- Why should we not steal?
- Lesson of Achan

NINETH COMMANDMENT 63

- What is lying?
- What are the causes of lying?
- Why should we avoid lying?
- How to avoid lying
- Lesson of Ananias and Sapphira

TENTH COMMANDMENT 72

- What is coveting?
- Lesson of Ahab and Naboth's Vineyard

CONCLUSION 79

GOD'S MERCY, LOVE AND FORGIVENSS THROUGH JESUS 81

ABOUT THE AUTHOR 84

The Ten Commandments

What are the Ten Commandments?

These Commandments were engraved on stone tablets and given to Moses by God on Mount Sinai. These Commandments are the heart of the law in the Old Testament.

How and from where did we get the Ten Commandments?

Long ago the Israelites were God's special people. He gave them the Ten Commandments. The Israelites lived in tents around Mount Sinai. Moses was the leader of God's people. One day God said to Moses, "Tell the people to get ready. They must wash themselves and wash their clothes. In three days I will come down to them. I will come to the top of Mount Sinai and talk to them."(Exodus 19:10)

By doing this, the people were preparing to hear important words coming from God himself. That is why we dress up or make sure that we have clean clothes on the day we go to church. It shows our respect to God.

On the third morning after Moses had spoken to God, the Israelites were busy making their breakfast when all of a sudden there was a large rumble and a flash of light over the mountain. Anyone who was still sleeping was startled and woke up immediately.

Everyone went out to look and just over the mountain there was lightning and thunder. There was a very thick cloud that hung over the mountain covering the top. The mountain shook and the sound of trumpets could be heard getting louder and louder.

Moses went up the mountain to hear from God once again. This time God told Moses, "Go down to the people and tell them not to follow you up the mountain. The mountain is a special place because I am here." So Moses warned the people not to touch or get too close to the mountain.

After that Moses went back up the mountain. This time he stayed there for 40 days and 40 nights. God sure had a lot to tell him. God wanted to instruct the people on how to live. By following His rules, they would have less sadness in their lives. God wanted to protect them.

This is exactly like when parents give us rules to protect us such as when they teach us that we must look both ways before we cross the street or that we must not hit our siblings. They give us rules because they love us and know what's best for us. They also want us to have a good time with each other.

What are we supposed to do with the Ten Commandments?

We need to know them and show them.

Deuteronomy 5:1 states, "Israel, listen to me. Here are the rules and laws I'm announcing to you today. Learn them well. Be sure to follow them."

There are laws everywhere, and once they are in place for everyone to follow, things are much easier. There are laws at school, at home, and on the road. It's important to put on a seatbelt in the car or have a booster seat so we can be safe in case the car has an accident. Drivers need to stop at a red light and go when there's a green light .We need to cross the road when the walking sign lights up. There are rules for skiing in a safe way and for running in a safe way and in the right place. These rules help protect us.

Exactly like this, God gave us rules so that when we obey these rules, we will be safe and at the same time, we will also have fun as we go through life. When we obey these rules, God has wonderful plans for us. (Jeremiah 29:11)

God is not looking to trap us so we can fail the rules. He understands that we are only human and how hard it is. That's why He sent his son Jesus to take the punishment for our sins.

Many times, He gives us consequences for our disobedience, not to punish us but to turn our attention back to Him so we can come to Him and say that we are sorry.

When parents let us face the consequences of our mistakes, we will be sure to remember that the last time we refused to clean our mess, parents had to cancel friends from coming over, or some toys were taken away. God does the same thing to remind us when we don't stay on the right path.

Think about a mother eagle carrying her baby beneath her wing and teaching it to fly. She does not let go of the baby eagle until it is ready to fly. It's the same with God's laws. They are to teach us to fly and when we fall short, He picks us up.
(Parents look up eagles with your young ones in the encyclopedia or internet.)

Purposes of the Ten Commandments:

1. To help strengthen our relationship with God.

After Adam and Eve were sent out of the Garden of Eden, people's relationship with God was broken. This caused them to forget about God, so they started worshiping false gods, but God wanted people to know about Him once again and have a relationship with Him. In order to do this, He gave the laws to people so they could know who He was and how they should act towards him and each other.

2. To expose our sin.

We are all sinners and it's the law that shows us how sinful we are and our need for God through his son, Jesus.

3. To keep us safe.
God made these laws to keep us safe just as our parents put a safety fence around the backyard to keep away wild animals and to protect us from running into the street when playing. Every little detail in our lives involves God. He must be put before all else. God wants to hear us pray and speak to Him before we call our best friends, turn on the television or play video games.

4. It also helps us define right and wrong.
The Ten Commandments have helped shape the basic moral laws of many nations. That is why someone goes to jail for stealing and murder. In courts they still use an oath before testifying. This oath states, " Do you solemnly swear or affirm that you will tell the truth, the whole truth, and nothing but the truth, so help you God?"

Questions:

1. Do you have laws or rules at school?

2. What are some of the classroom rules?

3. What are some rules in your house?

4. Why do we have the Ten Commandments?

Prayer:

Lord, we know that you don't expect us to be perfect but you want us to do our best. Please restore to us the joy of your salvation and make us willing to obey you. -Psalm 51:12

Bible Verses:

Deuteronomy 6:6 "The commandments I give you today must be in your hearts."

Romans 3:19-20 "Now we know that whatever the law says it speaks to those who are under the law, so that every mouth may be stopped, and the whole world may be held accountable to God. For by works of the law no human being will be justified in his sight, since through the law comes knowledge of sin."

Matthew 22:37 "Jesus replied, 'Love the Lord your God with all your heart and with all your soul. Love him with all of your mind.' This is the first and most important commandment. And the second is like it. 'Love your neighbor as you love yourself.' Everything that is written in the Law and the Prophets is based on these two commandments."

Matthew 5:17 - "Do not think that I have come to abolish the Law or the Prophets; I have not come to abolish them but to fulfill them.

Activity: Marble analogy

You will need: 1 marble, 1 flat plate and 1 bowl.
Place the marble on the plate and rotate the plate in a circular motion. Slowly increase the speed of the rotation and attempt to keep the marble on the plate. This will become increasingly harder and the marble will eventually fall off the plate.

Now place the marble in the bowl and rotate the bowl in a circular motion. Slowly increase the speed of the rotation while keeping the marble in the bowl. The sides of the bowl permit you to increase the speed of the marble without losing control.

Lesson: The plate does not have boundaries. In the same manner, without boundaries we, like the marble, may spin out of control. God's commandments are like the sides of the bowl. At first glance they appear to be barriers. However, they in reality, act as guidelines that keep us safe and permit us to move more freely through our lives.

Did you know that Adam and Eve's disobedience broke God's law? Did you know that sin separated them from God? Everyone born after them was sinful and separated from God too.

1. YOU SHALL HAVE NO OTHER GODS BEFORE ME.
EXODUS 20:2-3

In this commandment, we learn of God's love by knowing that God is the only true God. He is the one who created us, loves us, and is powerful enough to help us. He is the only God we will ever need. Therefore, why would we want any other gods?

What does it mean to have no other gods before God?

It means to put God first and love Him before anything else.
Before all the fun, before television, video games, and the sports we play or watch. Nothing should take God's place in our lives. Love God first, and then other things second.

As you enjoy everything you do, remember to talk to God. Thank Him for all the gifts He has given you and talk to Him just as you would talk to a friend. By doing this, it helps you put God first before the fun.

What is a god?

A god is something that you want so badly or love so much that you can't remember your love for God the Father.

When God says, "You shall have no other gods before me," it means you can love other things, (television, video games, movie stars and many more.) but not to the point where you're almost worshiping them.

What happens when we put God first?

1. When we put God first, we get to know Him better and what He wants us to do. Spending more time with our friends, helps us to know them better. This is the same way with when it comes to God. When we spend time with Him, we get to know Him better.

2. When we focus on God first before everything else, all other things work out the way God wants them to.

3. He will lead and direct us in everything that we do, according to Proverbs 3:5

4. When we put God first, He does not let us down at any time. Let's take a look at one of the most amazing lessons in the faithfulness of God through His servant Daniel.

DANIEL IN THE LIONS' DEN

(Daniel 6:1-28)

This is a story about Daniel. He actually came to Babylon years ago with Shadrach, Meshach, and Abednego. Darius was the new king of Babylon and he was smart . He picked a hundred and twenty of the very best people in his kingdom to help him rule. He picked three of them to be in charge. Daniel was one of those three men.

The king respected and liked Daniel because he was a hard worker. He decided to put Daniel in charge of the whole country.

The other servants of the king were very jealous of Daniel and they constantly tried to find something that would get him in trouble with the king. No matter how hard they tried, they couldn't find anything bad or wrong about Daniel. He was always true to the king and always prayed to God three times a day.

Finally these men said to each other, "We can't find anything wrong with Daniel. The only way we can get him to disobey the king is if we make a law against his God. "For we know he can't stop worshipping his God." So they went to king Darius and said, "O great king, you are so wonderful that no one should pray to anyone but you."

The king said, "That sounds like a great idea!" Then the men continued, "All of your workers have agreed that this should be done and that anyone that prays to any other god should be thrown into the lion's den."

The workers lied and said that everyone who worked for the king agreed, but of course they never talked to Daniel because they knew he wouldn't agree. The king didn't know this, so he made the law and it couldn't be changed.

When Daniel heard about the new law, he did what he always did. He went home to a room upstairs and opened the windows that looked out over the city. Three times that day he went down on his knees and prayed to God just like he always had.

These men went to Daniel's house and found him praying. They ran straight to the king and told him, "Your worker, Daniel, is ignoring your command. We have seen him praying to his God three times today."

When the king heard this, he was very sad. He really liked Daniel and he didn't want him to die. He tried everything to get the law changed to stop Daniel from being thrown in the lions' den, but the men came to him and reminded him that the law could not be changed and that Daniel would have to be punished.

The king said to Daniel, "May your God who you serve rescue you!"

The king couldn't eat or sleep that night because he was so worried for Daniel.

Very early the next morning, he rushed back to the lions' den. As he got closer he shouted, "Daniel, servant of the living God. Has your God whom you serve continually, been able to save you from the lions?" Maybe the king didn't expect an answer, but Daniel replied.

"O king, live forever! My God sent his angel, and he shut the lions' mouth. They have not hurt me because I have done nothing wrong."

King Darius was very happy and immediately ordered that Daniel be removed from the den. There wasn't even a scratch on him.

The king gave a command that the men who tricked him into getting Daniel in trouble be thrown in the lions' den and they were eaten by the lions.

King Darius wanted the world to know that the God of heaven had protected his faithful servant Daniel, so he wrote a letter that ordered everyone to worship the living God who rescued Daniel from the lions.

Daniel loved his job, but he had decided to put God first when they told him he couldn't pray to God anymore. We're on the winning side when we put God first. God loves us so much and He stays by our side all the time, especially if we put Him first.

Once again, Daniel was faithful. And God was able to show us that He is always able to do great and wonderful things.

Questions:
1. What is a god?
2. What happens when we put God first?
3. What did Daniel do when he was told he couldn't pray to God?
4. How did God show himself to Daniel in the lions' den?
5. What things can you think of that could become a god or idol to you?
6. Is there anything taking God's place in your life?

Prayer:

Dear Lord, I thank you for making me so special so that I can worship You. I want to put You first in my life. Help me, Lord, so that I can depend on You more than anything else. Sometimes I get so distracted with the things that I like to do, yet I know that You are more important because you made me so that I can worship You. I know that you do not expect me to live for you in my own strength, and You understand when I make mistakes, but I trust that your strength will hold me. Amen.

Bible Verses:

Daniel 3:1-30 (The Fiery Furnace)

Romans 8:28 "And we know that in all things God works for the good of those who love him, who have been called according to his purpose".

Genesis 1:27 "So God created mankind in His own image. In the image of God He created them. Male and female He created them."

Deuteronomy 6:5 " Love the Lord your God with all your heart, soul and strength."

Matthew 6:33 "But seek first His kingdom and His righteousness, and all these things will be given to you as well."

Philippians 4:19 " And my God will meet all your needs according to the riches of his glory in Christ Jesus."

Matthew 6:24 "No one can serve two masters. Either you will hate the one and love the other, or you will be devoted to the one and despise the other. You cannot serve both God and money."

Proverb 16:3 " Commit to the Lord whatever you do, and He will establish your plan."

Activity:
Do a treasure hunt. Parents, hide chocolate golden coins all over the room. Also hide

2-4 bigger silver treasures with sheets of paper inside, saying "**ALWAYS PUT GOD FIRST.**" Have each sheet of paper written with one of the four words.

1. **ALWAYS**   2. **PUT**   3. **GOD**   4. **FIRST**

(You can make your own silver treasures using aluminum foil) Children should try to find them, but they can't eat them right away!

Hold up a balled up piece of aluminum foil so they can see it.

As the kids find all the gold and silver, let them put it in the center of the table or on the floor in a circle.

Once all the coins are found, open the silver balls and find the four pieces of paper hidden inside. Put them in order. They will spell out: **ALWAYS PUT GOD FIRST.**

Have them give the gold coins back. They will have to wait to have the gold coins for another day or they will have to decide if they choose to give them to some others who may need them more. This can be their introduction to sacrifices and tough choices.

2. YOU SHALL NOT MAKE OR WORSHIP IDOLS

EXODUS 20:4-5

What is an idol?
It is something that replaces God.
God wants us to recognize that He is the only true God who created all things. He doesn't want us to let anything or anyone become more important to us than He is.

While we may not have real carved stone idols, whatever it is that we build up to be more important than our God can be an idol. Today we are tempted with all kinds of things that can take the place of putting God first. This could be video games, sports, money or movie stars that become our focus.

We can make these things gods of our lives, and if we focus on them too much they begin to control us and everything we do. They become idols or the "carved images" that take our focus away from God.

God is very clear in His word as He reminds us, "You shall not make for yourself an image in the form of anything in Heaven above or the earth beneath or in the waters below. Do not bow to or worship any statues of gods." (Exodus 20:4-5)

You shall not make yourself a graven image.

What does it mean to have an image in the form of anything?

It means to twist our understanding of God to be like a created being. We can do this by making a statue of wood or stone and calling it God or by simply saying, "what I want God to be."

God has shown Himself to us in the Bible alone. To change what He is in our own imagination is worshipping an idol. This situation is related to the first commandment. God wants our love, and He doesn't want us to bow down and worship a statue just because we can't see Him. God is the only one that we should pray to.

"God made animals, plants, the world, the sun, the moon, and the stars (Genesis 1:14-19). They are all beautiful and wonderful. It is foolish to worship anything in creation, when we could instead be worshiping the God who created them." And yes, God is bigger than our imagination!

When reading in the Old Testament, we might not understand why the people would bow down before idols they had made with their own hands. Surely, they did not think that these were living and powerful! But we make a similar mistake by placing too high a value on our own "idols" such as money, relationships, appearance, and power. Though not bad in themselves, these can become things we worship if we let them have too much importance in our lives. God is jealous for our hearts.

What happens when we worship Idols?

1. It breaks the first Commandment of not putting any other gods before God the creator.
2. It keeps us separated from God. Without faith in God alone, we cannot be forgiven for our sins. Romans 3:22 says, "We are made right with God by putting our faith in Jesus Christ."
3. It takes away our worship, which belongs to God.

Let's journey through a great story from the Bible where God's prophet, Elijah, meets with the 450 prophets of the false god, Baal. (1 Kings 18:15-39)

Also read 1 Kings 16:29-18:14

ELIJAH ON MOUNT CARMEL

(1 Kings 18:16-45)

This story is about a prophet named Elijah. Elijah was a regular man who made mistakes, was sometimes afraid, yet when it really mattered, he trusted God. Elijah did amazing things with God's help and God did amazing things for Elijah.

God's people, the Israelites, were divided into two kingdoms during that time. They were often tempted to copy the worship practices of their neighbors in the land of Canaan.

Ahab was the king over part of Israel. His wife, Jezebel, worshipped a false god named Baal. Ahab built a temple and altars where he worshipped Baal. Ahab turned his back on God and worshipped an imaginary creature that was made up by people. This did not make God happy.

"He did more to arouse the anger of the Lord, the God of Israel, than all the kings of Israel before him." (I Kings 16: 33).

God sent Elijah to tell king Ahab that there would be no rain in his kingdom for the next three years. Elijah did this, then left, and could not be found for three years and not even a single drop of dew would fall until Elijah had called for it. After so many days went by the plants started to die, and without both food and water, the animals started to die and people would start to die, too. God still took good care of Elijah.

It wasn't God's plan for His people to suffer. He just wanted them to turn away from their false gods and worship Him again. The King's wife, Jezebel, worshipped false gods and also decided to kill all the prophets of God, the creator.

After getting King Ahab's attention with three years of no rain, God sent Elijah back to the king. When Ahab called Elijah a "troublemaker," Elijah said that it was the king himself who brought trouble upon Israel by leading them in worship of false gods. Elijah asked that all the 450 false prophets of Baal meet on Mount Carmel in the presence of all the people.

Elijah spoke to all the people and told them that it was time for them to make a decision. He said that if God was the one true God, they should follow Him, but if Baal was the one and only god, they should follow him. The people fell quiet.

Elijah had two bulls killed for a burnt offering. He invited the prophets of Baal to go first, preparing their altar and doing everything but starting a fire. He said, "I will do the same with the other bull. Then let the prophets of Baal pray to their god, and I will pray to the Lord, and the god who answers by sending fire—He is God."

The prophets of Baal prayed all morning until noon, dancing and cutting themselves trying to get their god to act, as they called, "Baal, answer us!" But nothing happened. They finally gave up.

Elijah then set up an altar for the Lord, and put wood and the bull upon it. He put twelve stones on the altar-one for each of the twelve tribes of Israel. He placed firewood on top of the stones and dug a ditch around the altar. Then he ordered the wood to be soaked with water three times, making it more difficult to burn. The altar was drenched with water. He prayed to the Lord, "Answer me Lord, answer me, so that these people will know that you, the Lord, are God and that You are bringing them back to Yourself." God sent fire from heaven that not only consumed the sacrifice, but the water in the trench around it and the stones of the altar itself! The people exclaimed, "The Lord is God. The Lord alone is God!"

Then Elijah told Ahab to go eat and drink, because rain was on its way. Elijah climbed to the top of the mountain. He bent down low and prayed to the Lord. Then Elijah sent his servant to look out over the sea, but his servant returned saying that he didn't see anything.

Elijah sent him back six more times. Finally, the servant returned and reported to Elijah that he could see a tiny cloud the size of a man's hand. Elijah knew what this meant and he sent word to Ahab that the rain was coming.

This story shows God's power, the one true God against the false gods. It also shows the power of God in stopping the rain to punish the sins of the people and their king, and then ending the drought when the people turned to Him asking for forgiveness. God's mercy is always shown throughout the Bible as He continues to save His people whenever they turn to Him. And every time they do so, He is willing to forgive them, and still continues to forgives us as well.

Like the people of Israel in Elijah's day, we need to be reminded to confess, "The Lord is God; the Lord alone is God!"

Jesus taught his followers that idol worship happens when material possessions become more important to us than God (Matthew 6:24).

Along the same theme, the Apostle Paul stated that we should worship the Creator, not created things. (Romans 1:18-25)

In the story of Elijah on Mount Carmel, we learn that God was angry when King Ahab and Queen Jezebel worshipped idols and encouraged the citizens of their land to worship idols, too.

Why should God alone be worshipped?

1. He deserves the glory.
2. We worship God because we enjoy Him. (Psalm 100)
3. God has done so much for us.

We worship God in different ways. We worship him by singing, reading the Bible or praying, acts of kindness and in so many other ways.

2 Kings 18:38-39

We see God's blessings for the people who worshipped Him as they are written in the Bible:

Abraham became the father of many nations.

God considered David a man after His own heart.

Questions:
1. What were the idols in this story?
2. How many priests of Baal offered sacrifices?
3. How many prophets of God offered sacrifices?
4. Why do you think Elijah wanted the altar to be so wet?
5. Which God answered the sacrifice?
6. What did the prophets of Baal do as they prayed to Baal?
7. How do you think the people felt when they finally got rain after spending three years with no rain?
8. What is an idol?

Prayer:

God, so many times I choose to do things that I want and I do not put You first.

Help me to love and trust you always, to be brave when I am with friends who do not know You so that I can tell them about You and Your love.

Help me to always choose You first above all the fun things I enjoy. You are more important in my life than everything I have in this world. Amen!

Bible verses:
Isaiah 42:8 - "I am the Lord, that is my name! I will not yield my glory to another or my praise to idols."
Psalm 115:4-8 "But their idols are silver and gold, made by human hands. They have mouths, but cannot speak, eyes, but cannot see. They have ears, but cannot hear, noses, but cannot smell. They have hands, but cannot feel, feet, but cannot walk, nor can they utter a sound with their throats. Those who make them will be like them, and so will all who trust in them."

Isaiah 40:25-26 "To whom will you compare me? Or who is my equal?" says the Holy One. Lift up your eyes and look to the heavens: Who created all these? He who brings out the starry host one by one and calls forth each of them by name. Because of his great power and mighty strength, not one of them is missing.

Deuteronomy 6:5 "Love the Lord your God with all your heart, with all your soul, and with all your strength."

Activity:

Items needed:

Plastic pitcher or bucket (be sure the container holds as many cups of water as the number of kids).

-Water, tray, a cup, a rock, and a red permanent marker

Preparation: Pour a cup of water for each child.

Hand each child a rock and a marker. Ask the children to think about what takes up a lot of their time, attention, and money. Examples could be, TV, video or computer games, sports practice, or playing with friends. Have the children write or draw those things on their rocks. Use a red permanent marker to draw several large hearts on the pitcher, or use heart stickers and place the pitcher on the tray. Hand each child a cup of water.

Explain to the kids that the pitcher is like an empty heart. Fill this heart with God. When it is their turn, they should pour water into the pitcher and say, "God deserves first place in their heart because..." Then ask them to tell something about who God is. For example, as I pour my water in, I'll say, "God deserves first place in my heart because he is my *Creator or King.*"

Let each child have a turn until the pitcher is nearly full. Check out the following passages for more of God's qualities: Psalm 104:24 and Proverbs 3:19.

Our hearts are full of the goodness of God, but sometimes other things try to crowd into our hearts. Ask each child to say what they drew on their rocks and then they must place the rock into the water.

As the children add their rocks, the water will overflow. When they have finished, ask;

What happened to the water? Why?

How is this similar to our own hearts with God?

How can we keep our hearts full of God so He has the first place?

Conclude by all saying the second commandment.

"You shall not make any idols"

3. USE GOD'S NAME WITH RESPECT
EXODUS 20:7

God's name is Holy and important and His name is only to be said in a nice way. Today people use God's name without regard for His power and majesty. His name is His identity and we reveal a lot of how we feel about Him by the way we use His name. We should always respect His name and use it properly.

(Leviticus 11:44-45; I Samuel 2:2; I Peter 1:15, 16)

A name is more than a word; it is always associated with a person. A name in the Bible is an expression of a person's character and communicates something of what that person stood for. The Jews considered God's name so holy that they would not even say it or spell it. They would not even use it in prayer just so they would not misuse it. Instead they would substitute other words for it.

Worship and praise of His name is a proper use of His name. If you use God's name in cursing, it is an abuse of His name.

God listens to us when we call out to Him in prayer. Therefore, we need to be careful not to abuse that amazing privilege.

You shall not misuse the name of the Lord your God, for the Lord will not hold anyone guiltless who misuses His name.
(not to take God's name in vain) EXODUS 20:7

What does it mean to misuse God's name?

It means using God's name in an incorrect, disrespectful way without a specific purpose. God does not take it lightly when we do that. We are responsible for every word that comes out of our mouths, whether it is good or bad.

When we take God's Name "in vain", we make it seem like God is not important to us. That's one reason why we don't want to say things like, "Oh God" or "Oh my God" in a casual way. We should not use swear or curse words or say God's name when upset. A better way to remember may be to only say God's name when we are actually talking about God.

God wants us to use His name when we are talking to Him, or telling others about Him in a nice way. To use His name in these other ways is very disrespectful and hurts God to hear it.

James 5:12 - "Above all, my brothers and sisters, do not swear- not by heaven or by earth or by anything else. All you need to say is a simple "Yes" or "No." Otherwise you will be condemned."

Why Should We Respect God's name?

1. He is the name above all names.
2. Because God is holy, even His name is to be respected.
3. He is the creator of heaven and earth. Genesis 1:1

Why would you find it offensive if others were to treat your name disrespectfully? We all want good and honorable things associated with our names because our names are reflections of who we are. A strong relationship is based upon respect. One of the most important ways to respect God is by thinking highly of His name. He tells us not only to obey Him but also to hold His name as holy.

King David was a man after God's own heart. What was his attitude toward God's name? Read Psalm 145 to find out.

How do you think a person will treat Christ's name when he or she realizes that salvation is only through Jesus' name and that God will answer prayers in His name. (John 20:31, Acts 2:21 , John 16:23)

What names of God are revealed in the Bible?

"Elohim" means the Almighty or God the Omnipotent.

"Jehovah" is the common spelling of the Hebrew name of God which means the Eternal God. He lives forever and His character never changes.

"Jesus" means Savior.

"Christ" means the Anointed as were priests, prophets and kings in Israel.

Each name or title reveals something of God's character or divine nature. Find the name or title of God in each of the following scriptures. What does each name or title reveal about God?

What does each name reveal about His relationship to us?

Exodus 17:15, Exodus 15:26, 1Samuel 1:3, Psalm 7:17, Revelation 19:16, Revelation 19:11

What are some ways in which we don't respect God's name?

1. Making a false promise or vow using God's name. Jesus tells us to just use a simple "YES" or "NO" instead of making a promise. Also look at Matthew 5:37 and Leviticus 19:12.
2. Using God's name when we are mad and start cursing someone. (Psalm 139:20)
3. Using God's name carelessly.
4. Using God's name in worship with needless repetition and mouthing words without a deep sense of reverence or concentration.

This commandment requires that we honor God's name.

Did you know that names have meaning? In Bible times they used namse for specific meanings. (At times your friends will call you BFF.)

Hosea had to name his children different names as God commanded. Jesus' name. John the Baptist and so many other examples in the Bible show that people named their children or locations with special meaning or reasons. (Hosea 1:4-11), (Matthew 1:21)

Questions:

1. What kind of words do you think come from a clean heart?
2. What do we need to do to have clean hearts?
3. What does it mean to misuse God's name?
4. How can we use God's name in a respectful way?

Prayer:

Heavenly father, "May the words of my mouth and the meditation of my heart be pleasing to You oh Lord, my Savior". (Psalm 19:14)

Help me to use my lips to praise you. Clean my heart so that I can speak of your name with respect always. "You know every word I am going to say before I even say it." Help me to have good words come out of my mouth. For I am weak and you are strong. Thank you for your love and how you are very patient with me. Amen.

Bible verses:

Psalm 138:2 " I will bow down toward your holy temple and will praise your name for your unfailing love and your faithfulness, for you have so exalted your solemn decree that it surpasses your fame."

Matthew 12:34-35 " You brood of vipers, how can you who are evil say anything good? For the mouth speaks what the heart is full of.[35] A good man brings good things out of the good stored up in him, and an evil man brings evil things out of the evil stored up in him."

Activity: Tell your child how you chose his/her name and share any special meaning the name holds.

For a caregiver, encourage children to ask their parents how they got their name and any special meaning the name holds.

4. KEEP THE SABBATH HOLY
EXODUS 20:8

What is the Sabbath?

It means "time to rest". It also means "seventh".

Remember the Sabbath day to keep it holy."

The Sabbath is a sign between God and his people. As Ezekiel 20:12 tells us; " Also I gave them my Sabbaths as a sign between us, so they would know that I the LORD made them holy."

This commandment reminds us to rest one day a week and save it for God. It is a blessed and holy day. Some people have the Sabbath on different days but Sunday is the most recognized Sabbath day for Christians.

When we keep the Sabbath holy, we're showing respect for God because He is Holy.

God knows we work, but He also knows we need rest.

God wants us to take one day of the week and rest. When God made the world in six days, He rested on the seventh day. This gets harder when you get older because there always seems to be something to do, but remember God commands us to take a day off. We work for six days in a week and rest on the Sabbath day to reflect on what God did for us. To observe a day of rest and worship reveals just how important God is to us. (Ecclesiastes 9:10)

How can we keep the Sabbath holy?

1. Going to church to worship the Lord with other people who love Him.
2. Visiting the sick or lonely, and taking care of emergencies when they come. Luke 14:1-5 shows us that it is important to take care of emergencies on the Sabbath. We can go to the hospital if we get hurt, or if we are sick. We can help those in need. We should always plan ahead if it is possible, but sometimes accidents happen and people get sick, and we have to deal with these situations. God understands that and allows us to care for these things.
3. Resting from our work, studying God's word, praying to Him and thinking about all the things He is doing for us. It is a day of rest from doing the regular things that we might do on the other six days. (Deuteronomy 5:14)

4. Being happy and not sad. We should rejoice in the Sabbath and bring joy to the House of God. The Sabbath is a gift that God made for us! We were not made for the Sabbath. (Isaiah 58:13-14). Also read Mark 2:27.
5. Spending the day with our family, church family and friends. Most parents organize special treats and activities for their children to do on the Sabbath. It is all right for children to play on the Sabbath, walking in nature, writing letters, reading through family history and going to the park or other outside places to enjoy God's natural creations. Learning about the One True God and His laws can be fun too. These are usually things that we do not do on the other six days, as it is a special time. While working on the Sabbath day is generally discouraged, there are certainly professionals such as doctors and policemen that need to work on that day.

It's important to prepare for the Sabbath. What day would be best for preparation?
The day before the Sabbath is the day we should prepare for the Sabbath. We call this the preparation day. (Exodus 16:5)

MANNA FROM HEAVEN

(Exodus 16:4-28)

While God's people, the Israelites, were in the wilderness, they had to eat somehow and God provided food for them. The food was called manna and quail. Every day they had to gather just enough food for the day. If they took too much food, it would get spoiled the next day, and it would smell too bad for them to eat. This was another reminder that God wants us to worry about one day at a time, instead of worrying about the upcoming days. God was teaching His people to trust Him to supply their needs.

The only time they were allowed to take food enough for two days was the day before the Sabbath. It is then that food would not get spoiled and smell really bad. God reminded them that they were to rest on the seventh day.

Even though some people still disobeyed Him and went out to look for food on the Sabbath, they didn't find anything.

It's also good for us to do all our work on Saturday as we get ready for Sunday so that when Monday comes, we feel refreshed and ready to go back to school/work. If we work continuously for seven days a week, it is hard for us to even tell what day of the week it is, and it is also hard to have a fresh mind when you are so tired.

Questions:

1. What does the Sabbath mean?
2. What are some things we can do on the Sabbath?
3. When is a good day to get all your chores done so you can rest on the Sabbath?
4. How much food were the Israelites supposed to get the day before the Sabbath?
5. What happened to the food if they collected more than they needed during the other six days?

Prayer:

Thank You God, that You want me to rest after working hard all week long, going to school, doing homework and chores like house cleaning and laundry. Help me to honor this special day and keep it holy. May you remind me always if I am doing things I should not be doing on this special day. Teach me all the things I need to know about the Sabbath. I want to live for You, and that Is one of the reasons you made me. In Your precious name, I pray! Amen.

Bible Verses:

Exodus 16:5 "And it shall come to pass, that on the sixth day they shall prepare that which they bring in; and it shall be twice as much as they gather daily."

Exodus 16:23 'He said to them, "This is what the LORD has commanded: 'Tomorrow is a day of solemn rest, a holy Sabbath to the LORD; bake what you will bake and boil what you will boil, and all that is left over lay by to be kept till the morning."

The Bible includes a great story of how God took the Sabbath seriously. This story is found in Exodus 16:4-28

Nehemiah 10:31 "When the neighboring peoples bring merchandise or grain to sell on the Sabbath, we will not buy from them on the Sabbath or on any holy day. Every seventh year we will forgo working the land and will cancel all debts"

Jeremiah 17:22 "Do not bring a load out of your houses or do any work on the Sabbath, but keep the Sabbath day holy, as I commanded your ancestors."

Genesis 2:2-3 " By the seventh day God had finished the work he had been doing so on the seventh day he rested from all his work. God blessed the seventh day and made it holy because on it he rested from all the work of creating that he had done.

Hebrews 10:24-25 "And let us consider how we may spur one another on toward love and good deeds, not giving up meeting together, as some are in the habit of doing, but encouraging one another and all the more as you see the Day approaching.

Acts 20:7 " On the first day of the week we came together to break bread."

Activities:
Plan and perform a family musical recital. Arrange to go and perform the recital at a nursing home or children's hospital on a Sunday or on your Sabbath.

Make cards one Sunday afternoon and take them to a nursing home to help make the patients there feel encouraged.

5. HONOR YOUR FATHER AND MOTHER
EXODUS 20:12

Honor means to respect. It also means to obey. This Commandment tells us to love and obey our parents immediately, completely, and sweetly with a happy attitude. Our parents are valuable because they are God's gift to us just as we are God's gift to them.

Sometimes we might think we know what is best and even get frustrated because our parents will not let us do something. Remember that parents were once kids as well. They are only trying to keep us safe and prevent us from making the same mistakes they have already made. They know what is best for us. Think of all the things your parents do for you.

They protect you from so many dangers without you even realizing it. They provide you with things you need like food and clothing. They even give you extra things you do not need but they know you would like to have such as; toys, bikes, special treats and more.

"Honor your father and mother, so that you may live long in the land the Lord your God is giving you." Exodus 20:12

What are some ways you can honor your parents?

1. By obeying them, being kind to them and speaking to them with respect.
2. Having a good attitude and not talking back. God gives us parents to protect us and give us what we need. It can be very hard for them to do that if we do not listen to them.
3. Loving and listening to your parent's advice.

We should also honor those who take care of us and teach us as our parents would.

When you respect and obey God by honoring your parents your life will be long. This is the one Commandment to which God adds a promise. (Exodus 20:12)

Why should we obey our parents?

1. It pleases God when we follow His law.
2. It creates a good relationship between you and your parents. Instead of your parents spending so much time repeating what you should have done, they could use that time to play with you or do something fun with you.
3. When we obey we learn skills to use that would be useful to us when we are with strangers, teachers and friends. If we are used to using good manners at home, it will be very easy to apply them when we're away from home.

As with all the Commandments, only Jesus lived in perfect obedience. Look up to Jesus. We can trust in His righteousness to cover our shortcomings. Only His grace can change our naturally rebellious hearts to rightly honor our earthly parents as well as our Heavenly Father.

God knows that if we love and obey our parents it will be easier for us to love and obey Him as well.

HOW JESUS HONORED HIS PARENTS
(Luke 2:41-52)

Every year Jesus' parents went to a special celebration in the spring. That year, as usual, Mary, Joseph and Jesus traveled to Jerusalem for the celebration. They went with a big group of friends and family.

When the celebration was over, Mary , Joseph and the rest of the group started traveling back to their home. After a while Mary and Joseph realized that Jesus was nowhere to be found. They asked all their friends and family, but no one had seen Jesus.

Mary and Joseph rushed back to Jerusalem. They looked everywhere for Jesus. Can you imagine how upset Mary and Joseph must have been? Finally, after 3 days, they found Him. He was in the temple talking to the leaders. He and the leaders had been there talking together the whole time! The leaders were amazed at what Jesus knew.

When Mary found him she said, "Son, why did you do this to us? Your father and I were very worried about you!"

Jesus asked, "Why did you have to look for me? You should have known that I would be in my Father's house", but they did not understand what He meant.

Jesus went with them to their home in Nazareth and He obeyed them. He listened and did what His parents asked Him to do. Jesus continued to grow up. People liked Him and He pleased God, too.

We learn from this story in the Bible that Jesus loved His parents and did what they said. He obeyed them. He did not talk back to them or ignore them. He honored them. God wants us to honor our parents too. Isn't it great to know that Jesus lived like us? He knows what it's like to grow up because he grew up too. He knows what it is like to have parents because He had parents too. Jesus lived with people like us and understands everything we go through.

Questions:
1. What does it mean to honor your parents?
2. Which commandment tells you to honor your father and mother?
3. What is God's promise for those who honor their parents?
4. What are some ways in which you can honor your parents?
5. Why should you honor your parents?
6. Who set a perfect example for us?

Prayer:
Our Father in heaven, You are holy. Your Commandments are wise.
You ask us to honor our parents. Please help us to understand what that means. Help us to obey You by honoring and respecting them.
In Jesus' name, we pray. Amen.

Encourage children to thank God for their parents in their own words. Let the children tell you why they should honor you or why they should honor their parents.
For example: "Thank You, Lord, for my Mom and Dad". I honor them because they read me bed time stories.

Bible Verses:

1 John 4:20 " Whoever claims to love God yet hates a brother or sister is a liar. For whoever does not love their brother and sister, whom they have seen, cannot love God, whom they have not seen."

Ephesians 6:1-3 "Children, obey your parents in the Lord, for this is right. "Honor your father and mother" which is the first Commandment with a promise, "so that it may go well with you and that you may enjoy long life on the earth."

Proverbs 23:22 "Listen to your father, who gave you life, and do not despise your mother when she is old."

Proverbs 1:8 "Listen my son, to your father's instruction and do not forsake your mother's teaching."

Colossians 3:20 "Children, obey your parents in everything, for this pleases the Lord."

Deuteronomy 5:16 "Honor your father and your mother, as the Lord your God has commanded you, so that you may live long and that it may go well with you in the land the Lord your God is giving you."

Activities:

Mom and Dad can share a personal story of a time when they did not show respect and honor to their parents, how that made them feel at the time and how God has changed their lives for the better.

Play

Father Says Game:

Instead of Simon Says, you could play Father Says. You could substitute acting out realistic directions rather than the typical silly commands. Some examples would be:

Father says clean your room (pretend to clean)

Father says go to bed (lay down and pretend to fall asleep)

Father says do your homework (pretend to do homework)

Father says help your mother (act like they are helping Mom with something)

Father says stand up straight (practice good posture)

Father says eat your pizza (pretend to eat)

Father says brush your teeth (pretend to brush teeth)

Jesus had an earthly father named Joseph. We know that Jesus was the only child to ever perfectly obey his father. So, Jesus can forgive our sins and help us become better children to our parents.

6. YOU SHALL NOT MURDER
EXODUS 20:13

What is murder?

Murder means to take someone's life. But Jesus says, we are not even to call someone a bad name. That's the same thing as murder because we are not concerned about their feelings being hurt by our words. Mathew 5:21-22

Hating or having bad feelings about someone is the first step toward wanting to hurt or get back at them.

Now imagine for a minute if everyone in the whole world obeyed this rule like God wants us to. We probably would not have any prisons, and we would all get along well with one another.

It is hard to show love to your neighbor and tell him about God if he is dead. It is not right for you to take another's life. Murder is always a selfish act where someone believes that something in their life is more important than another person's life. God calls us to give up our lives for others, not take others lives for ourselves (John 15:13).

It is not good to destroy the feelings of others, their confidence, sense of self-worth or dreams. Do not engage in any behavior that hurts someone else.

Let us visit this story from the Bible to help us better understand murder.

CAIN AND ABEL

(Genesis 4:4-15)

In this story, Cain is the older brother . Cain was a farmer who planted fruits and vegetables. Abel was a shepherd and took care of sheep. One day it happened that Cain and Abel brought gifts to God to thank Him for all the good things he had done for them. They built an altar for a sacrifice.

A sacrifice is when you give something away that you would have liked to keep for yourself. When Sacrificing to God, You give Him your very best in order to please Him and make Him happy.

During offering and thanking God for His provision Cain gave some of his fruits to God. He didn't give his best though. On the other hand, Abel chose the best of his animals to give to God and thank Him for what He had done.

Since Abel was very generous with his gifts, God was extremely pleased with what Abel had given, but He was not very happy with Cain's gifts.

Cain became very angry and felt sad. God asked him, "Why are you angry with such a sad face? If you do what is right, you will be accepted, but if you do not do what is right, bad thoughts will ruin your life. You must learn to control them."

And even though God loved both brothers as much as anyone could ever be loved, Cain thought that God loved Abel more than He loved him. From that day on, Cain began to think mean things about his younger brother. He kept thinking and the more he had these thoughts, the harder it became for him to stop and one day, he planned a terrible thing.

He said to his brother on a bright, sunny morning, "Abel, come with me out into the fields."

"Sure," Abel said, because he loved his big brother and also trusted him. When Cain got Abel out where nobody could see or hear them, he picked up a rock and used it to kill his little brother, Abel. Later that day, God found Cain working in the hot sun. God said to him, "Where is your brother ?"

"How should I know?" Cain answered. "Am I supposed to take care of my brother all the time?" But God knew the terrible thing Cain had done to Abel. God said to Cain, "What have you done? Your brother's blood cries out to me from the ground."

Now you are under a curse and driven from the ground which opened its mouth to receive your brother's blood from your hand. When you work the ground, it will no longer yield its crops for you. You will forever be a restless wanderer on this earth."

"Lord, this punishment is too hard for me!" Cain said. "My relatives will try to kill me when they hear of what I have done. I will always be running forever." So, God put a mark on Cain to protect him. When anyone saw it, they would know not to kill him because God was watching. One day Cain left his only home and family because of the evil thing he had done. Adam and Eve lost not just one son, but two and Cain lost his family. Worse than that however, God would not be with him anymore. That would be the hardest thing of all. Cain went away and lived in the land of Nod, east of Eden.

Cain would not have thought of killing his own brother if he had only been obedient to God. God had already told him to do what was right. While he was angry, he also needed to not act on his anger by making a bad choice. Every sin has a consequence and even though God is kind and loving, He is also just.

Cain was punished by not ever being able to relax or rest forever again. Moving from one place to another and not finding peace was a hard way to live.

With God's mercy, Cain was not to be touched or killed by anyone else. God told him that whoever killed him would have more serious consequences than Cain was given.

Genesis 4:4-15

Questions:

1. What does sacrifice mean?
2. What does murder mean?
3. Why did Cain kill Abel?
4. What was Cain supposed to do for God to accept his gifts?
5. Why was God pleased with Abel's gifts?

Prayer:

Lord God, help me to respect life by being obedient to You, putting You first, others second and myself last. Help me to be kind, polite and to control myself when I am angry and to depend on you if I fail to control my anger. In Jesus' name I pray. Amen.

Bible Verses:

Exodus 20:13 "You shall not murder."

Leviticus 24:17 "Anyone who takes the life of a human being is to be put to death."

Revelation 21:8 "But the cowardly, the unbelieving, the vile, the murderers, the sexually immoral, those who practice magic arts, the idolaters and all liars—they will be consigned to the fiery lake of burning sulfur. This is the second death."

Activities:

Sacrifice: Have kids go through their toys and choose one of them to give to the needy or someone they know who will enjoy it. It has to be one of the special toys they really like.

Make a poster together on how special each family member is, to show uniqueness and respect for life. (Reference Verse- Psalm 139:14 .....I am fearfully and wonderfully made...")

7. YOU SHALL NOT COMMIT ADULTERY

EXODUS 20:14

When a man and a woman get married, they promise to love only each other and not to love anyone else in that same special way. They are to stay married for the rest of their lives.

God blesses marriage between a man and a woman.

When two people get married, God gives them to each other. This is very special! (They would not want to go out and get somebody else!) He wants us to keep ourselves special for our spouses.

Committing adultery is breaking a promise that was made when getting married. When a husband and wife break this promise, it breaks up families and the hearts of so many involved.

The Bible tells how in the Old Testament, Joseph worked for a married man. The man's wife wanted to love Joseph the way she loved her husband, but Joseph said, 'No!' and ran away. You must also run away from people who want you to break your promises to God and to others.

You don't need to worry about a marriage promise until you are much older. For now, focus on loving your family. Someday, if God's plan for you is to be married, He will bring that special person into your life at the right time.

God sees marriage as a very important commitment. In marriage, two people of different families come together to become one family. It is very similar to an adoption. Like God's adoption of us, it lasts forever and so should marriage. You know that no matter what, God will always love you and will never give up on you. That is how God wants us to see marriage and God does not want married people to be unfaithful to each other.

Let's visit a story in the Bible you may have heard before :

DAVID AND BATHSHEBA

(2 Samuel 11:1-17)

God chose David to be the king of His people. He loved God very much. However, there was a time when David disobeyed God.

In the spring, David's men went into battle, but David stayed at home instead of going with his men. One night, he saw a beautiful, married woman named Bathsheba. David thought she was so beautiful that he invited her secretly to come into the palace. That night, David and Bathsheba did a very wrong thing and sinned against God. Several months later, Bathsheba sent a note to David telling him that she was pregnant with his son! David was hopeless and felt the need to cover up his sin. Instead of confessing his wrongs to God, he acted like God did not know and he tried to cover up the wrong.

He asked Bathsheba's husband Uriah, to come back from battle and stay with his wife. Unfortunately, his plan did not work. Instead of staying with his wife, he slept outside by the palace. David still did not want to confess his wrong doing. He came up with an awful plan. He asked his general to put Bathsheba's husband on the front lines of battle where he would be killed. Sure enough, Uriah died in battle. When Bathsheba heard the news, she was very sad.

After she had a time of mourning, she became David's wife. She gave birth to a baby boy. God was not pleased with David's sin and lies. God sent a special man named Nathan to talk to David about his sin. Nathan had plenty of courage. He was not sure how David would react to his news from God. Nathan obeyed God and shared a story to help David see the horrible thing he had done.

Nathan told David a story about a rich man that had much and a poor man that had one little lamb. When the rich man needed a lamb for a feast, he took the lamb of the poor man instead of his own. David was angry. He couldn't believe that someone would do such a thing. Then Nathan told David that he was like the rich man in the way that he took another man's wife. Nathan told David that God knew of all the wrong things that he had done. David wept and told God that he was sorry for all the sins that he had committed. He even wrote a beautiful psalm to tell God how sorry he was for all the wrongs he had done. Nathan told David that God forgave him but ,however, because of his sin, his son would die. David had to deal with the consequences of his sin.

Exactly as Nathan said, David's son became very ill and died. David was very sad about this but knew that God still loved him.

God cared for David and blessed him and his family. God forgave his sin and made him clean again.
Not only did David break the 7th commandment, but he also lied and murdered an innocent man.

Questions:

1. In your own words, explain adultery.
2. What other sins did David break when he committed adultery?
3. What did David do when Nathan gave him a message from God?
4. What was David's consequence for his sin with Bathsheba?

Prayer:
Dear Lord God Almighty, thank you for giving me a wonderful family that loves me. I pray that you can be with my dad and mom in their marriage always. I also trust that when I am an adult, you have someone special for me if it is your plan for me to be married. Help me to wait patiently upon you every day and to honor you in everything that I do. Amen.

Bible Verses:
Ecclesiastes 9:9 " Enjoy life with your wife, whom you love, all the days of this meaningless life that God has given you under the sun- all your meaningless days. For this is your lot in life and in your toilsome labor under the sun."

Proverbs 5:18 " May your fountain be blessed, and may you rejoice in the wife of your youth."

Matthew 19:5-6 "For this reason a man will leave his father and mother and be united to his wife, and the two will become one flesh; So they are no longer two, but one. Therefore what God has joined together, let no one separate."

Matthew 5:28 " But I tell you that anyone who looks at a woman lustfully has already committed adultery with her in his heart."

Activity:

Parents or leaders, talk to your children about keeping promises and being a loyal friend. Talk to them about things they can relate to. Ask them what a promise is. Ask them if they have ever broken a promise. Ask if anyone has ever broken a promise to them and find out how they felt about that?
You can even go into detail and ask them to talk about some of their favorite promises of God in the Bible and how He fulfilled them. Discuss with them in a manner similar to the following passage, "What if I promised to take all of you to the park, then give you pizza for lunch, and then your favorite cookie for dessert." You were really excited and got ready. How would you feel if I just changed my mind and said I didn't feel like it?"

Go a little closer to the Commandment and ask them how they would feel if they played with a friend all year, who promised to sit with them in school and save them a seat. Then after that they meet another kid they thought was cool and sat with them instead? How would they react? How do they feel about promises?

Teach them about how you go into marriage and how you make a promise to one person to spend the rest of your life with them. You can't just change your mind and then go with someone else.

8. YOU SHALL NOT STEAL
EXODUS 20:15

What is stealing?

It means to take something that belongs to someone else without their permission or taking without asking. Someone who steals is called a thief. The heart of a thief is never to share or to give to others.

Robbing a bank and shoplifting are not the only ways to steal. It could be copying answers from another person's school paper or it could be stealing another person's chance to win by cheating in a game. Keeping extra change is also another way of stealing.

Why should we not steal?

1. It goes against God's nature. God is honest, true and loving toward others. God also wants us to trust Him to give us what we need, but when we steal, we miss out on God's care, and it gives us a bad image in the eyes of God and people.
2. God promises to provide for all of our needs. If we steal things from others, we are denying God's ability to provide for us. In Matthew 6:26, God promises to care for us since we are more valuable to Him than the birds that He feeds. God also took care of Elijah when he was fed by ravens, by an angel, and by a widow. God also took care of John the Baptist when he lived in the wilderness.
3. We lose the opportunity to be a good neighbor because you cannot be friends with someone you steal from . God wants us to work for what we have and get.

There was a time in Israel before Jesus was born where whole families were responsible and punished for the sins of an individual family member. Do you think it would be fair if you were punished for something your brother or sister did?

How serious can stealing be? Let us take a look at another story from the Bible.

ACHAN

(Joshua 7:1-24)

After Moses died Joshua became the leader of the Israelites. It was Joshua who led the people over the Jordan River and into the Promised Land. They had to fight many battles to get their land back from the Canaanites. The first battle they fought was the Battle of Jericho. Have you heard of this? They marched around the city seven times, blew the trumpets and all the walls came tumbling down! Joshua had ordered the people to take nothing from the city for themselves. If they found any silver, gold, bronze or iron they were to give these to the Lord so that they could maintain the house of God. The soldiers were not to take anything for themselves.

After they entered the city of Jericho the soldiers went through the rubble, collecting the gold, silver, bronze and other riches. Every soldier brought everything he found to the treasury of the Lord. Everyone, that is, except one man, Achan, who disobeyed.

When Achan saw a beautiful robe and some silver and gold among Jericho's treasures, he desired them for himself and decided to steal them when no one was looking, Achan took the robe, silver, and some gold and buried them underneath his tent!

When Joshua found out about this, he was shocked and horrified! This was a very serious crime! Who would dare to steal from God?

Joshua sent some men to search Achan's tent and they found the stolen goods hidden there. God told Joshua he had to punish Achan's whole family for what he had done!

This, I am sure, made Joshua very sad, but he had to punish Achan for disobeying God's command. Joshua put Achan and his whole family to death and then burned all of his possessions. The Israelites saw that disobeying God had serious consequences.

What a shame that Achan's whole family had to suffer because of Achan's greed. Are you not glad you do not have to be put to death when one of your family members sins against God?

Since then, God, in His mercy, has changed those customs.

Ezekiel 18:20 "The person who sins is the one who will die. The child will not be punished for the parent's sins, and the parent will not be punished for the child's sins. Righteous people will be rewarded for their own righteous behavior, and wicked people will be punished for their own wickedness."

Stealing is always wrong. It is never right. God says that if you are a thief you must be punished.

Did you know that there are places in this world today that have some very serious punishments for crimes. In some countries if you are caught stealing, they will cut off one of your fingers! If you were caught stealing twice, how many fingers would you have left? (8)

That is how we are going to remember the 8th Commandment. " **Do not steal!** "

People also rob God when they fail to give their offerings, called "tithes" to God. A tithe is 10 percent of our money. We are told to give 10% back to God.

Why should we give God money? God doesn't need our money or our things. What He needs is us. The process of giving blesses and changes us.

It costs a lot to keep the church going. They have rent to pay, supplies to buy, electricity and many other bills to pay. God expects people to help out with those expenses.

When we don't give our tithe to God, we're stealing from Him.

Questions:

1. Robbing a bank and shoplifting are not the only ways to steal. Can you think of other ways people steal things?
2. What happened to Achan's family when Joshua found out that he had kept a beautiful robe, some silver and gold for himself instead of giving it to the Lord?
3. When you sin, who is responsible? Who is the one that deserves to be punished?
4. What is a tithe?
5. Why should we give God money?

Prayer:

Dear Lord Jesus, thank You for leaving Your home in heaven. All of us have sinned. All of us have stolen in big ways or little ways. Please help us to obey Your eighth commandment, "You shall not steal." We want to be givers, not takers. In Jesus' name! Amen.

Bible Verses:

Ephesians 4:28 "Anyone who has been stealing must steal no longer, but must work, doing something useful with their own hands, that they may have something to share with those in need."

Matthew 6:26 "Look at the birds of the air; they do not sow or reap or store away in barns, and yet your heavenly Father feeds them. Are you not much more valuable than they?"

Exodus 20:15 "You shall not steal."

Malachi 3:8 "Should people cheat God yet you have cheated Me! But you ask, 'What do you mean? When did we ever cheat You?' You have cheated Me of the tithes and offerings due to Me."

Activities:

Encourage kids to give some of their allowance earned at home to God. For example, money earned by doing extra chores or baby sitting in the neighborhood or even something they could share. God asks us to give to Him 10 percent of everything we receive. That's what a tithe is: 10% means for every ten pennies we get, we give back one penny to God. That is not much, is it?

Bring in a pile of pennies, scatter them around a table and count out ten pennies in a row. For older kids, challenge them to figure out how many pennies is a tenth of 50 cents and/or a dollar, and so forth.

Let us be "givers" and not "takers!"

Get three jars. Every time a child gets money they can divide it into three equal parts - one for each jar. 10% will be the tithe for Church, in the second jar put the spending money, and save 10-20% in the third jar. This is a great way to learn budgeting as well.

9. YOU SHALL NOT LIE
EXODUS 20:16

What is lying?

Lying is when you are not telling the truth or not telling the whole truth. God is very clear in giving this commandment; *"You shall not give false testimony against your neighbor." Exodus 20:16*

Truth is truth no matter what. God is truth; and when we lie, we go against His character.

Deuteronomy 32:4 tells us that God is perfect and does no wrong.

False testimony means lying or not telling the whole truth.

God does not want us to give a false testimony of anyone. We should not put our own blame on others nor should we cover up the blame for others. If you do something wrong, you should not blame your brother or sister. Instead, you should admit to what you have done. If you know of someone else who has done wrong, you should not cover it up. Helping others get away with doing wrong keeps them from getting right with others and with God.

What are the causes of lying?

1. It is so easy to lie especially if you want something from someone or if you want to avoid a consequence from your parents for doing something wrong. We learn about how Jacob with the help of his mom, lied to his dad, Isaac. He pretended to be Esau so he could steal his brother's blessing. In Genesis 27:18-35)
2. Some people lie to avoid causing problems for others or even just to avoid hurting their feelings. For example, Abraham moved to a foreign land; He told his wife Sarah to tell people that she was his sister. Otherwise someone might kill him to take her as a wife. Genesis 12:11-13
3. Some people lie to cover-up or hide something. When people sin or commit other acts and they want to hide from others, they often tell lies. In Genesis 37:28-33, Jacob's sons lied to him about their brother, Joseph, by saying that he had been killed by a wild animal instead of telling the truth which was that they sold him as a slave because they were jealous of Joseph.

4. Pride can be a cause for lying. Often people tell lies because they want others to think they are better than they really are. The lie Ananias and Sapphire told in Acts 5:1-9 was motivated by pride. Other people were giving sacrificial gifts to the church, and they wanted people to think they had made a bigger sacrifice than what they had. The Pharisees were prideful and also hypocritical because they pretended to be religiously devout in order to get the favor of people. (Matthew 6:2,5,16)
5. Some people begin to lie for various reasons, but then it just becomes a way of life or a habit. They lie even when there appears to be no real purpose in it.

Jeremiah 9:4,5 - People could not trust anyone else because everyone would deceive his neighbor. They would not speak the truth; they taught their tongue to speak lies.

John 8:44 - Jesus said regarding Satan:, "There is no truth in him. When he speaks a lie, he speaks from his own resources, for he is a liar and the father of it." Satan influences men to lie. When we tell lies, we have followed the influence of Satan, but the ultimate problem is in our own hearts.

Why should we avoid lying?

1. **Lying Harms Other People.** After Jacob stole his brother's blessing, their relationship was ruined .
Genesis 37:33-35 - "When his sons deceived him, Jacob grieved and mourned for many years believing his son Joseph really had died. Later, his sons were sorry for the grief they had caused."
2. **Lying Influences Others to Sin.** Liars set a bad example for others which can lead them to lie as well.
Proverbs 29:12 - "If a ruler pays attention to lies, all his servants become wicked."
3. **Lying tends to feed on itself.** The more some people tell lies, the more other people become encouraged to tell lies as well. We see a pattern in the Bible of how children learned to practice lying from their parents. Jacob learned it from his mother and his uncle Laban, and his sons learned it from Jacob.
4. **Lying Leads to Loss of Respect and Confidence.** Who can trust someone who is known to tell lies? People want friends they can trust and rely on. If you want good people to respect and trust you, don't lie.
Psalm 40:4 - "Those who love God do not respect those who turn aside to lies."

Young people need to learn this lesson early. If you lie to your parents or friends about where you go or what you do, it ruins your relationship. Some complain, "Why don't you trust me?" "I only told one lie." That's all it takes to destroy trust. After that, your parents and friends can never know when you are being truthful and no one will believe you.

5. **Lying separates us from God and condemns us eternally.**
   Remember that lying is twice in the list of things that God hates.
   If we want spiritual fellowship with God, we must love truth, speak truth, and remove lying and deceit from our lives.
   Proverbs 12:22; 6:16-19 - "Lying lips are an abomination to the Lord, but those who deal truthfully are His delight."
   Psalms 5:6 - "God will destroy those who speak falsehood. He abhors the bloodthirsty and deceitful man."
   Revelation 21:8 - "All liars will have part in the second death, the lake of fire."

How to avoid lying

1. **Love truth and hate lies.** Don't just mildly dislike lies, but practice telling the truth. If you continually remind yourself of the terrible consequences of lying, this should keep your motivated enough to avoid lying .
2. **Fill your heart with truth.** To be speakers of truth, we must fill our hearts with truth, especially with God's word.
   John 8:32 " Then you will know the truth, and the truth will set you free."
3. **Stay far from falsehood.** We must both fill our hearts with truth and reject lies and deceit. Don't harbor falsehood in your heart and it cannot be expressed in your speech.
   Proverbs 30:8 - "Remove falsehood and lies far from me. Don't see how close to error you can get; stay "far" from lying."
4. **Avoid People and influences known to lie or deceive.** Often we end up telling lies because we hang around liars. We listen to their lies, and we learn to imitate their evil.
   Proverbs 17:4 - "An evildoer gives heed to false lips; A liar listens eagerly to a spiteful tongue. When we listen to other people's falsehoods, we are tempted to speak them ourselves."

It is always better to tell the truth, and while you're at it, don't do anything that would make you want to lie. Usually parents know when you're lying anyway, and if you don't get caught, God sees and hears everything and He knows.

There are many times in our lives when we may be tempted not to tell the whole truth. If we have done something wrong, leaving out details might seem like a convenient way to stay out of trouble.

Let us read one of the examples from the Bible about lying and how serious it is to God.

ANANIAS AND SAPPHIRA
(Acts 5:1-11)

Ananias and Sapphira were married. They had some land they could sell. They saw that the Christians were giving money to Peter who was a follower of Jesus. Ananias and Sapphira thought they could impress Peter by giving him some money too, so they sold the land and took only a part of the money to the disciples and laid it at their feet. "Look!" Ananias told them, "I sold some of my land and here is all the money I made!" Peter said to Ananias, "Why have you kept part of the money from the sale? It was your money, under your own control, so why have you come up with this lie in your heart? You haven't lied to men, but to God! And do you think God wants us to lie?"

Well, right after Ananias heard this from Peter, he fell down dead! Some men came and carried the body of Ananias out of the temple. They were amazed and a little scared by what had happened.
About 3 hours later Sapphira came to Peter. She hadn't heard what happened to her husband yet. Peter asked her, "Tell me, is this the price you and Ananias got for the land?" She answered, "Yes, that's how much we sold the land for." Peter asked her why they had agreed together to test God. Peter told her to look at the feet of the men that buried her husband because they would carry her out, too! Immediately, Sapphira fell to the ground dead. The men came to carry her out and they buried her next to her husband.

People heard about Ananias and Sapphira from far away! They heard about how they had lied to Peter and most importantly, lied to God. Ananias and Sapphira died instantly because of their lies!

Great fear came upon all the church and upon all who heard about this.
Many Christians learned that day that God sees and hears everything that we say and do.

Are you not glad that God does not strike us down instantly now? Jesus already took the punishment for our sins.

Questions:

1. Has anyone ever lied to you? How did you feel?
2. What are some causes of lying ?
3. What are some reasons we should not tell lies?
4. What does lying mean?
5. What happened to Ananias and Sapphira when they lied?
6. How can you avoid lying?

Prayer:

Dear Heavenly Father, "Keep falsehood and lies far from me; give me neither poverty nor riches, but give me only my daily bread. Otherwise, I may have too much and disown you and say, "Who is the LORD? Or I may become poor and steal, and so dishonor the name of my God." (Proverbs 30:8-9)

Bible Verses:

Psalm 24:3-5 -"Who will stand in God's holy place? Those who have clean hands and a pure heart. Those who have not lifted up their souls to falsehood and have not sworn deceitfully. This is the one who will be blessed by the Lord."

Psalm 119:163 - "I hate and abhor lying, but I love Your law."

1 Corinthians 13:6 - "Love does not rejoice in iniquity, but rejoices in the truth."

Psalm 5:6 "You destroy those who tell lies. The bloodthirsty and deceitful LORD, you detest."

Psalm 15:2 "The one who abides in God's tabernacle is he who speaks the truth in his heart. "

Psalms 51:6 "You desire truth in the inward parts, and in the hidden part You will make me to know wisdom."

Proverbs 25:18 "A man who bears false witness is like a club, a sword and a sharp arrow."

Psalm 101:7 " No one who practices deceit will dwell in my house; no one who speaks falsely will stand in my presence."

Proverbs 19:22 " What a person desires is unfailing love; better to be poor than a liar."

Psalm 52:2-4 "The deceitful tongue loves evil more than good and lying rather than speaking righteousness. "

Exodus 23:7 "Have nothing to do with a false charge and do not put an innocent or honest person to death for I will not acquit the guilty."

Activity:

Have kids go through the first 9 Commandments and what each Commandment means.

10. YOU SHALL NOT COVET
EXODUS 20:17

What does Covet mean?

Covet means to want what others have and to wish to have things that someone else has. The Tenth Commandment ties all the others together. *"You shall not covet your neighbor's house. You shall not covet your neighbor's wife or his male or female servant, his ox or donkey, or anything that belongs to your neighbor." Exodus 20:17*

If this happens, you will end up breaking many of the commandments. King David, as we read in Commandment 7 coveted Uriah's wife, and therefore broke the 10th commandment, which led him to break the 7th Commandment of adultery. He then stole someone's wife, which broke the 8th Commandment. He then had Uriah killed breaking the 6th Commandment.

Another way to remember this commandment could be, "*You shall not want what others have.*" Like a new toy, a game, an X-Box or a tablet. There can always be something that we want to get, but it's important to remember that these things are not really important. God is more important.

Let's look at a very interesting story from the Bible about a very rich king named Ahab and what happened to him when he started coveting someone's vineyard.

AHAB & NABOTH'S VINEYARD

(1 Kings 21)

There was a man named Naboth from Jezreel, who owned a vineyard in Jezreel next to the palace of King Ahab of Samaria. King Ahab wished to own this vineyard. One day he said to Naboth, "Since your vineyard is so close to my palace, I would like to buy it to use as a vegetable garden. I will give you a better vineyard in exchange, or if you prefer, I will pay you."

Out of obedience to God's orders, Naboth refused to sell the vineyard. Back when God handed out the land to the twelve tribes of Israel, He forbid them to sell or give their part of the land to another tribe or family (Leviticus 25:23).

So, Ahab went home angry because of Naboth's answer. He refused to eat, but lay down on his bed with his face to the wall. His wife, Jezebel, asked why he was so upset. Ahab answered her, "I asked Naboth to sell me his vineyard or even trade it, but he refused!"

Jezebel said, "Is this how the King of Israel acts? Rise up and eat something! Enjoy yourself. I will get you the vineyard of Naboth." Jezebel came up with an evil plan. She wrote a letter to the leaders of the town where Naboth lived. In her letter she said, " Let the word be given out that a meeting of the men of Jezreel is to be held, and set Naboth up before all the people. Have two men who will help lie that they heard Naboth curse God and the king. Then take Naboth out, and the people will throw stones at him until he is dead."

Since the people were so scared of Queen Jezebel, they did as she had commanded. As a result, Naboth was stoned to death. When Jezebel heard the news of Naboth's death, she said to Ahab, "You know the vineyard Naboth wouldn't sell you? Well, you can have it now! He's dead!" So, Ahab immediately went down to the vineyard of Naboth to claim it. He took his two captains with him. Just as they were riding in the vineyard Elijah, the prophet suddenly stood before them. He had a very important message from God for King Ahab. The Lord was going to punish Ahab for being a part of Naboth's murder. Ahab was surprised when he saw Elijah.

Elijah gave Ahab this message, "Because you gave yourself over to do evil in the sight of the Lord, in the place where dogs licked the blood of Naboth, dogs shall lick up your own blood. "I am going to bring horrible trouble on you. I will destroy your children after you. I will cut off every male in Israel who is related to you.

It does not matter whether they are slaves or free.

You have made me very angry. You have caused Israel to commit sin."

Because your wife Jezebel has encouraged you to sin, she shall die and the wild dogs of the city shall eat the body of Jezebel by the wall of Jezreel." Ahab took Elijah's prophecy seriously. He realized how wicked he had acted and felt sorrow for his sin. He tore his clothes and put on black clothes.

This was a sign of mourning, as if someone had died. Ahab stopped eating and began to act very humble, seeking God's forgiveness. God sent another message to Elijah about Ahab. It said, "Have you seen how Ahab has made himself low in My sight? Because he has done that, I will not bring trouble on him while he lives. But I will bring it on his royal house when his son is king." God had already decreed a punishment - Ahab, Jezebel, and their sons would be destroyed. However, because Ahab finally bowed down to the Lord, and acted with humility, God would not punish Ahab's sons until after Ahab had died.

God had blessed Ahab by making him king of His own people, but Ahab turned his back on God by doing evil instead of what was right. The Bible says, "There was never anyone like Ahab. He gave himself over to do what was evil in the sight of the Lord. His wife Jezebel talked him into it. He worshiped statues of gods."

In time, all that God had spoken came to pass. Ahab died in battle when the Lord decided it should happen . Jezebel died in the exact way Elijah had prophesied. Eventually, all of Ahab's descendants were killed.

1 Kings 22:20, 37

1 Kings 21:23,

2 Kings 9:33-37

2 Kings 10:11

Notice that Ahab and Jezebel's sin brought terrible consequences for their children. They lived wicked lives in front of their children. Their children followed their wicked behavior, and they too, would be punished.

Even if Ahab did so much evil in the eyes of God, as soon as he humbled himself, God continued to show his mercy and grace upon Ahab by deciding not to punish him at once Ahab realized that he had done wrong in God's eyes and repented of his sin. Yet, even after all of the horrible things that Ahab had done, God showed mercy to him because he repented of his sin. God did not bring punishment to Ahab's sons while Ahab was alive. Even though God is just and must punish sin because He is holy, He is also completely loving, giving us every opportunity to turn from our sin, and turn to Him. God always wants us to turn to him and humble ourselves. God is not there to get back at us. He wants a relationship with us. That is why He created us.

Did you know that Adam and Eve always talked with God? In the beginning, in Genesis, we see the wonderful relationship that Adam had with God before sin entered the world.

Questions:

1. What does covet mean?
2. What is a vineyard?
3. Did Ahab tell the whole truth to his wife about the vineyard?
4. What are you struggling with lately?
5. Are you discontent with anything?

Prayer:

Dear Heavenly Father, Lord, thank You for providing for all my needs. Help me to keep my life free from the love of money and the materialistic things of this world. You have given me all I need, so help me to be content with what I have because You said in your word, "Never will I leave you, never will I forsake you". In Jesus' name I've prayed! Amen.

Bible verses:

James 4:2 "You desire but do not have, so you kill. You covet but you cannot get what you want, so you quarrel and fight. You do not have because you do not ask God."

Psalm 23:1 " The LORD is my shepherd; I lack nothing."

Philippians 4:11-13 "I am not saying this because I am in need, for I have learned to be content whatever the circumstances. I know what it is to be in need, and I know what it is to have plenty. I have learned the secret of being content in any and every situation, whether well fed or hungry, whether living in plenty or in want. I can do all this through him who gives me strength."

1Timothy 6:6-10 "But godliness with contentment is great gain. For we brought nothing into the world, and we can take nothing out of it but if we have food and clothing, we will be content with that.

Those who want to get rich fall into temptation and a trap and into many foolish and harmful desires that plunge people into ruin and destruction. For the love of money is a root of all kinds of evil. Some people, eager for money, have wandered from the faith and pierced themselves with many griefs."

Hebrews 13:5 " Keep your lives free from the love of money and be content with what you have, because God has said, "Never will I leave you; never will I forsake you."

Activities:

Make a blessing board. List all the things God has blessed you with. When you see all God has done for you, it will encourage you to be content and thankful to God for all the good things you have.

Start up a piggy bank and collect money to give away to the poor. Try to sign up with one of the organizations that help poor kids in other countries. They will send you letters in the mail with stories of other children and families. When you see how poor other people are, it will be a great way to see how blessed you are.

Some of the organizations are;

-Global Refugee International

- Compassion radio

-Compassion International (you get to adopt a child by sponsoring)

- Samaritan's Purse

-Feed the Children

-World Vision

There are so many other wonderful organizations. Pray and see what God lays upon your heart.

CONCLUSION

When you get a puppy to have for a pet, you have to train her/him to sit, come when called, and to walk on a leash especially when you live in the city. By training your puppy, you show you love him or her and you want her or him to be safe, especially at the times when you need to cross the road so he or she doesn't get hit by a car. God's laws are to keep us safe because He loves us.

When we obey God by following His commandments, not only will we be safe, it will also be easy for us to receive His blessings and to let Him pour out His love for us instead of constant discipline to get our attention.

(Deuteronomy 6:5 and Leviticus 19:18).

God's Ten Commandments show us how to love God and other people. They come out of God's love for us and they are all about love. Let's review the commandments in summary again. Read also Exodus 20:1-17.

The first four commandments teach us how to love God and the last six help us know how to love people.

1. HAVE NO OTHER GODS	6. DO NOT MURDER
2. HAVE NO IDOLS	7. DO NOT COMMIT ADULTERY
3. RESPECT GOD'S NAME	8. DO NOT STEAL
4. KEEP THE SABBATH HOLY	9. DO NOT LIE
5. RESPECT YOUR PARENTS	10. DO NOT COVET

There is another simple way to memorize the ten commandments by using your fingers. Visit this website; **http://www.myblessedhome.net**
Check under parenting and then Guiding young hearts, look up "fun ways to memorize the Ten Commandments."

Can you imagine how things would be in a world without laws if everyone did what they wanted? What a chaotic world that would be!

GOD'S MERCY, LOVE AND FORGIVENSS THROUGH JESUS

God will do whatever it takes to draw us to Himself because He loves us so much and doesn't want us to get hurt. Just as parents protect us and make sure we don't get hurt, they will do anything to have a good relationship with us.

We see that God had taken good care of the Israelites. He rescued them from slavery and helped them by taking them to the promised land. But His children continued to walk away from Him.

God continues to pursue them. He calls them and hasn't given up on them because of His love.

Isaiah 1:18 says, "Come now, let us settle the matter, says the LORD. "Though your sins are like scarlet, they shall be as white as snow; though they are red as crimson, they shall be like wool."

Lamentations 3:22-23 "Because of the Lord's great love we are not consumed, for his compassions never fail. They are new every morning; great is your faithfulness."

God is perfectly merciful, loving and kind. There is no greater proof of this than the fact that God sent His Son, Jesus, to pay for our sin and save us (John 3:16).

Just like Ahab, each one of us has done evil in God's sight, and we deserve to be punished by our just God.

Romans 3:23 " For all have sinned and fall short of the glory of God." Only our faith in Jesus takes our sin away and brings us back to God.

Exodus 34:6-7 "I am the Lord God. I am merciful and very patient with My people. I show great love, and I can be trusted. I keep My promises to My people forever, but I also punish anyone who sins. "

Like a good judge, God must punish sin. It would not be fair for a judge to allow someone to break the law and not punish him, but this makes God very sad because God loves people very much(Genesis 6:6) , (1 John 4:8).

Just as God forgave David's wrongs, King Ahab's wrongs and the constant forgiveness to His people the Israelites, as we can see in the Bible. He can forgive our wrongs too. God made a way to clean out the wrongs in our heart. God's Son, Jesus, took all our punishment for the wrongs we did when he died on the cross.

He was the substitute to pay for the sins we committed. Three days later, Jesus rose from the grave. If we believe in Him and trust Him with all our heart, He will clean out all the wrongs and forgive us.
He will help us live for Him and do things His way instead of our way.

As we read about King David, we notice that even if he did bad things, God still loved him and used him to do many great things. Also, God said of David: "He is a man after God's own heart." God gives us second chances to do right. In fact, with God's help, David wrote part of the book in the Bible called Psalms to remember that God promised that David's kingdom would never end. Jesus comes from David's side of the family. Read Matthew 1:1-16 to find out the details of Jesus' family.

Ezekiel 18:21 "But if wicked people turn away from all their sins and begin to obey my decrees and do what is just and right, they will surely live and not die. "

God is gracious and merciful. He's not willing that anyone should die in their sins. The sinner who comes to faith will be forgiven and given a brand new start. But, your old habits must change! You can't keep on stealing or lying. God expects you to obey all Ten of His Commandments!

Questions:

1. How many of the Commandments can you recite from memory? If you don't know them all yet, work on memorizing them.
2. Who can you share these Commandments with and tell about Jesus this week?
3. What is the greatest example of God's love for us?
4. After going through all the Commandments, which one is the hardest one for you?

Prayer:

Oh, how I love your law! I meditate on it all day long. Your commands are always with me and make me wiser than my enemies. I have more insight than all my teachers, for I meditate on your statutes. I have more understanding than the elders, for I obey your precepts. I have kept my feet from every evil path so that I might obey your word. I have not departed from your laws, for you yourself have taught me. Help me Lord! Amen. (Psalm 119:97-102)

Final Activity:

Using a brand new set build legos that are specifically for a certain category such as a car or any character.

Before you read the instructions, try building them to see if you can come up with the picture similar to the one on the box.

The next day or with time, try to build one following the instructions that come in a box.

This activity shows how hard it can be doing anything without instructions, rules or directions.

OR:

Using a new game you have never played before, play without reading the rules to the game. After that, try to follow the rules to the game and see how easy it is to play if you know the rules.

For discussions, join me on the Facebook group;
The Ten Commandments for Kids and Family Devotional

ABOUT THE AUTHOR

Rose Fresquez is a full-time wife and mother of three children living in Denver, Colorado. She has devoted her time to raising her children, Isaiah, Caleb, and Abigail while her husband, Joel, works outside the home. She is a former administrative assistant for the children and student ministry at her home church, Riverside in Denver. She currently helps with children's worship as well as leading prayer time. She loves to sing and uses her vocal talent to give praise to her Lord and Savior.

About the illustrators

Vladimir Medina Cebu is a Law Degree Graduate of the University of Saint La Salle, and a businessman. Being a visual artist, his other passion is making illustrations for children's books. Someday, it is his life-long dream to be in the courthouses as a lawyer, and working with accomplished authors, providing book illustrations for children around the world.

David Dodson has a AA degree in Art from College of the Canyons in Santa Clarita CA. He is a freelance artist and also works in the construction Industry.

Made in the USA
Monee, IL
25 September 2022

14472761R00055